The Flaxseed Goodness

Explore the Best of Flaxseed Recipes

BY: SOPHIA FREEMAN

© 2019 Sophia Freeman All Rights Reserved

COPYRIGHTED

Liability

This publication is meant as an informational tool. The individual purchaser accepts all liability if damages occur because of following the directions or guidelines set out in this publication. The Author bears no responsibility for reparations caused by the misuse or misinterpretation of the content.

Copyright

The content of this publication is solely for entertainment purposes and is meant to be purchased by one individual. Permission is not given to any individual who copies, sells or distributes parts or the whole of this publication unless it is explicitly given by the Author in writing.

My gift to you!

Thank you, cherished reader, for purchasing my book and taking the time to read it. As a special reward for your decision, I would like to offer a gift of free and discounted books directly to your inbox. All you need to do is fill in the box below with your email address and name to start getting amazing offers in the comfort of your own home. You will never miss an offer because a reminder will be sent to you. Never miss a deal and get great deals without having to leave the house! Subscribe now and start saving!

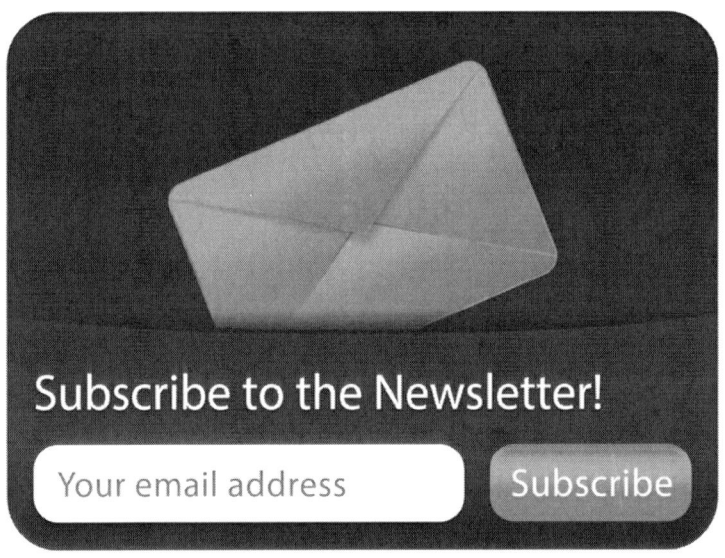

Table of Contents

Delicious Flaxseed Recipes 9

Chapter I - Snacks 10

    1) Rice Patties 11

    2) Onion Avocado Rings 14

    3) Battered Tofu 17

    4) Stuffed Olives 20

    5) Cheese Balls 23

Chapter II - Salads 26

    6) Potato and Cheese Salad 27

    7) Grilled Bread Salad 29

    8) Mayo Chicken Salad 31

    9) Tuna Salad 33

    10) Gouda Salad 35

Chapter III - Breakfast 37

    11) Egg Flaxseed Muffins 38

    12) Mushroom French-Toast.. 40

    13) Peanut Pancakes 42

    14) Cheese Rolls... 44

    15) Milk Flaxseed Oats 47

    16) Mustard Tuna Sandwich 49

    17) Flaxseed Coconut Cereal 51

    18) Ham Quiche 53

    19) Chicken Egg Toasts... 56

Chapter IV - Main Meal... 59

    20) Baked Portabella Mushrooms with Veggies 60

    21) Lettuce Rolls 63

    22) Pinto Bean Toasts 67

    23) Avocado Burger.. 69

24) Potato Pork Scramble 72

25) Stir Fried Teriyaki Salmon with Toasted Flaxseeds 75

26) Chorizo Flaxseed Curry 78

27) Baked Aubergine 81

28) Fried Chicken Fillet 84

29) Beef Taco 86

Chapter V – Soups 89

30) Chicken Cream Soup 90

31) Beef Rice Soup 92

32) Flaxseed Tomato Soup 94

33) Pork Mushroom Soup 96

34) Thai Tofu Bell Pepper Soup 98

Chapter VI – Desserts 100

35) Coffee Flaxseed Pie 101

36) Fruit Cream 104

37) Fruit Cupcakes 106

38) Banana Pecan Ice-cream 109

39) Flaxseed Caramel Toffee 111

Chapter VII - Shakes 114

40) Pineapple Shake 115

41) Cherry Shake 117

42) Mango Shake 119

43) Butterscotch Shake 121

44) Banana Shake 123

Chapter VIII - Smoothies 125

45) Pineapple Kiwi Smoothie 126

46) Plum Mango Smoothie 128

47) Banana Apple Smoothie 130

48) Passion Fruit Grape Smoothie 132

49) Very Berry Smoothie 134

About the Author 136

Author's Afterthoughts 138

Delicious Flaxseed Recipes

zzzzzzzzzzzzzzzzzzzzzzzzzzzzzzzzzzzzzzzzzzzzzzzzzz

Chapter I - Snacks

zzzzzzzzzzzzzzzzzzzzzzzzzzzzzzzzzzzzzzzzzzzzzzzzzz

1) Rice Patties

Fried boiled potato and rice patties with garlic powder!

Yield: 4

Prep Time: 30 minutes

Total Cook Time: 10 minutes

Ingredient List:

- 2 medium potatoes, peeled and mashed
- 2 cups boiled rice
- 1 small onion, finely chopped
- 1 tsp. paprika
- 1 tsp. garlic powder
- ½ cup flax meal
- 2 whole organic eggs
- Pomace olive oil for deep frying
- Salt and pepper to taste

ZZZZZZZZZZZZZZZZZZZZZZZZZZZZZZZZZZZZZZZZZZZZZZZZZZZZ

Instructions:

1. Combine potatoes, rice, onion, paprika, garlic powder, salt, and pepper. Mix well and divide the mix into 4 equal portions. Make 4 patties and set aside.

2. Combine flax meal, eggs, pepper, and salt in a large bowl. Mix well until all the ingredients are uniformly combined. Set aside.

3. Heat olive oil in abottom pan over medium-high heat. Evenly coat each patty with the prepared egg mix and put them into the pan. Fry until golden-brown and crisp.

4. Once done, remove the patties from pan with the help of a strainer and place it over a paper towel so that it can absorb the extra oil. Keep aside.

5. Serve hot with mayo.

2) Onion Avocado Rings

Avocado stuffed battered onion rings!

Yield: 10

Prep Time: 30 minutes

Total Cook Time: 10 minutes

Ingredient List:

- 10 onion rings
- 2 cups puree avocado
- 1 small onion, finely chopped
- 1 medium tomato, finely chopped
- ½ cup flax meal
- 2 whole organic eggs
- 2 tsp. lemon
- Pomace olive oil for deep frying
- Salt and pepper to taste

zzzzzzzzzzzzzzzzzzzzzzzzzzzzzzzzzzzzzzzzzzzzzzz

Instructions:

1. Combine avocado puree, onion, tomato, lemon juice, salt, and pepper. Mix well and keep aside.

2. Place the rings on a baking tray. Fill them with the prepared avocado mix. Then, put the tray in the freezer for 3-4 hours.

3. Combine flax meal, eggs, pepper, and salt in a large bowl. Mix well until all the ingredients are uniformly combined. Set aside.

4. Once rings are frozen, take them out the freezer.

5. Heat olive oil in a deep bottom pan over medium-high heat. Evenly coat each ring with the prepared egg mix and put it into the pan. Fry until golden-brown and crisp.

6. Once done, remove the rings from pan with the help of a strainer and place it on a paper towel so that it can absorb the extra oil. Keep aside.

7. Serve hot with mayo.

3) Battered Tofu

Egg battered tofu chunks with thyme!

Yield: 2

Prep Time: 10 minutes

Total Cook Time: 10 minutes

Ingredient List:

- ½ pound tofu, diced
- ½ cup flax meal
- 2 whole organic eggs
- ½ tsp. chili powder
- 1 tsp. garlic paste
- 1 tsp. dried thyme, ground
- Pomace olive oil
- Salt to taste

zzzzzzzzzzzzzzzzzzzzzzzzzzzzzzzzzzzzzzzzzzzzzzzzz

Instructions:

1. Combine flax meal, eggs, chili powder, garlic paste, thyme, and salt in a large bowl. Mix well until all the ingredients are combined. Set aside.

2. Heat olive oil in a deep bottom pan over medium-high heat. Evenly coat each piece of tuna with the prepared egg mix and put them in the pan with hot oil. Fry until golden-brown and crisp.

3. Once done, remove the fried tuna from pan with the help of a strainer and place it over a paper towel so that it can absorb the extra oil. Set aside.

4. Serve hot with mayo or ketchup.

4) Stuffed Olives

Battered olives stuffed with minced pork!

Yield: 10

Prep Time: 30 minutes

Total Cook Time: 10 minutes

Ingredient List:

- 1 cup minced pork
- 10 large green olives
- 1 small onion, finely chopped
- ½ cup flax meal
- 2 whole organic eggs
- Pomace olive oil for deep frying
- Salt and pepper to taste

ZZZZZZZZZZZZZZZZZZZZZZZZZZZZZZZZZZZZZZZZZZZZZZZZ

Instructions:

1. Combine minced pork, onion, salt, and pepper. Mix well and stuff the olives with this mixture. Set aside.

2. Combine flax meal, eggs, pepper, and salt in a large bowl. Mix well until all the ingredients are uniformly combined. Set aside.

3. Heat olive oil in a deep bottom pan over medium-high heat. Evenly coat each olive with prepared egg mix and put it into the pan. Fry until golden-brown and crisp.

4. Once done, remove the olives from pan with the help of a strainer and place it on a paper towel so that it can absorb the extra oil. Keep aside.

5. Serve hot with ketchup.

5) Cheese Balls

Fried ricotta and mozzarella cheese balls with garlic and paprika!

Yield: 2

Prep Time: 20 minutes

Total Cook Time: 10 minutes

Ingredient List:

- ½ pound ricotta cheese, grated
- 2 cups mozzarella cheese, grated
- ½ cup flax meal
- 2 whole organic eggs
- ½ tsp. paprika
- 1 tsp. garlic paste
- Pomace olive oil for deep frying
- Salt to taste

zzzzzzzzzzzzzzzzzzzzzzzzzzzzzzzzzzzzzzzzzzzzzzzzz

Instructions:

1. Combine ricotta and mozzarella cheese in large bowl. Mix well and divide the mixture into 10 portions. Make 10 balls using your hands and set aside

2. Combine flax meal, eggs, paprika, garlic paste, and salt in a large bowl. Mix well until all the ingredients are uniformly combined. Set aside.

3. Heat olive oil in a deep bottom pan over medium-high heat. Evenly coat each cheese ball with th prepared egg mixture, then put them into the pan. Fry until golden-brown and crisp.

4. Once done, remove the balls from pan with the help of a strainer and place it on a paper towel so that it can absorb the extra oil. Keep aside.

5. Serve hot with ketchup.

Chapter II - Salads

zzzzzzzzzzzzzzzzzzzzzzzzzzzzzzzzzzzzzzzzzzzzzzzzzz

6) Potato and Cheese Salad

Boiled potato and parmesan cheese salad with balsamic vinegar!

Yield: 2

Prep Time: 15 minutes

Total Cook Time: 0 minutes

Ingredient List:

- 2 cups parmesan cheese, grated
- 2 medium potatoes, boiled and diced
- ½ cup roasted flaxseeds
- 3 Tbsp. balsamic vinegar
- 1 small head of lettuce, chopped
- 2 medium tomatoes, finely chopped
- Salt and pepper to taste

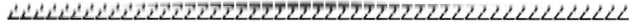

Instructions:

1. Combine all the ingredients in large bowl. Mix well.

2. Serve!

7) Grilled Bread Salad

Oven grilled bread bite salad with bell pepper, corn, and mint mayo!

Yield: 2

Prep Time: 15 minutes

Total Cook Time: 0 minutes

Ingredient List:

- 8-10 slices of bread
- ½ cup roasted flaxseeds
- 1 small head of lettuce, chopped
- 1 large green bell pepper, finely chopped
- 3 Tbsp. mint mayonnaise
- 1 cup corn kernels, chopped
- Salt and pepper to taste

Instructions:

1. Preheat the oven 350 °F.

2. Place the bread slices on the oven's grill. Bake until they turn crisp and brown.

3. Once done, remove the slices from the oven and let them cool down completely.

4. Once cool, chop the slices into bite size pieces.

5. Combine all the ingredients and grilled bread in large bowl. Mix well.

6. Serve!

8) Mayo Chicken Salad

Shredded roasted chicken salad with chili mayo and black olives!

Yield: 2

Prep Time: 15 minutes

Total Cook Time: 0 minutes

Ingredient List:

- ½ pound roasted chicken breast, shredded
- ½ cup roasted flaxseeds
- 1 small head of lettuce, chopped
- 2 spring onion, finely chopped
- 3 Tbsp. chili mayonnaise
- 1 cup black olive, chopped
- Salt and pepper to taste

Instructions:

1. Combine all the ingredients in large bowl. Mix well.

2. Serve!

9) Tuna Salad

Tuna flakes salad with radish, mustard sauce, and mayo!

Yield: 2

Prep Time: 15 minutes

Total Cook Time: 0 minutes

Ingredient List:

- 1, 5 oz. can of tuna flakes in olive oil, oil drained
- ½ cup roasted flaxseeds
- 1 small head of lettuce, chopped
- 1 cup radish, finely chopped
- 3 Tbsp. mayonnaise
- 2 Tbsp. mustard sauce
- Salt and pepper to taste

Instructions:

1. Combine all the ingredients in large bowl. Mix well.

2. Serve!

10) Gouda Salad

Boiled potatoes and grated gouda salad with french dressing!

Yield: 2

Prep Time: 15 minutes

Total Cook Time: 0 minutes

Ingredient List:

- ½ pound gouda cheese, diced
- 2 medium potatoes, boiled and diced
- ½ cup roasted flaxseeds
- 1 small head of lettuce, chopped
- 2 medium tomatoes, finely chopped
- 3 Tbsp. french dressing
- 1 medium cucumber, chopped
- Salt and pepper to taste

zzzzzzzzzzzzzzzzzzzzzzzzzzzzzzzzzzzzzzzzzzzzzzzzzz

Instructions:

1. Combine all the ingredients in large bowl. Mix well.

2. Serve!

Chapter III - Breakfast

zzzzzzzzzzzzzzzzzzzzzzzzzzzzzzzzzzzzzzzzzzzzzzzz

11) Egg Flaxseed Muffins

Baked flax meal and egg muffin packed with protein!

Yield: 6

Prep Time: 10 minutes

Total Cook Time: 15 minutes

Ingredient List:

- 6 whole organic eggs
- 1 cup flax meal
- 1 large onion, finely chopped
- 1 medium tomato, finely chopped
- Butter for greasing
- Salt and pepper to taste

zzzzzzzzzzzzzzzzzzzzzzzzzzzzzzzzzzzzzzzzzzzzzzzzz

Instructions:

1. Preheat the oven 350 °F.

2. Lightly grease 6 muffin molds with butter.

3. Combine all the ingredients in a large bowl. Mix well until all the ingredients are uniformly combined.

4. Then, pour prepared mix into the molds and place them on a baking tray.

5. Bake for 10-15 minutes or until eggs are cooked through and a skewer inserted in the center comes out clean.

6. Once done, remove the baking tray from oven to cool down a bit.

7. Serve hot!

12) Mushroom French-Toast

Bread slices battered with chopped mushroom and egg mix!

Yield: 2

Prep Time: 15 minutes

Total Cook Time: 15 minutes

Ingredient List:

- 4 slices of bread
- 4 whole organic eggs
- 1 cup white button mushrooms, finely chopped
- ½ cup flaxseeds
- 4 tsp. butter
- Salt and pepper to taste

zzzzzzzzzzzzzzzzzzzzzzzzzzzzzzzzzzzzzzzzzzzzzzzzz

Instructions:

1. Combine eggs, mushrooms, flaxseeds, salt, and pepper in a large bowl. Mix well until smooth. Keep aside.

2. Melt 1 tsp. butter in a non-stick pan over medium-high heat. Evenly coat each slice of bread with prepared mix and put it in the pan. Cook until both sides turn golden brown.

3. Repeat the same procedure and make 4 pieces of toast.

4. Once done, place the French toast slices on a serving platter.

5. Serve hot with ketchup!

13) Peanut Pancakes

A protein-licious breakfast with flax meal and egg whites!

Yield: 10

Prep Time: 5 minutes

Total Cook Time: 30 minutes

Ingredient List:

- 4 cups egg white
- 1 cup flax meal
- ½ cup peanut kernels, roughly chopped
- 2 Tbsp. sugar
- 1 tsp. vanilla essence
- 10 tsp. butter

zzzzzzzzzzzzzzzzzzzzzzzzzzzzzzzzzzzzzzzzzzzzzzzzz

Instructions:

1. Combine all the ingredients in a large bowl except for the butter. Mix well until smooth. Set aside.

2. Melt 1 tsp. of butter in a non-stick pan over medium-high flame. Pour in 1/10 of the prepared mix in the pan and cook until both side turn-golden-brown.

3. Repeat the same procedure and make 10 pancakes.

4. Once ready, place the pancakes on a serving platter.

5. Serve hot with condensed milk or maple syrup.

14) Cheese Rolls

Shallow fried bread rolls filled with ricotta cheese and rosemary!

Yield: 2

Prep Time: 20 minutes

Total Cook Time: 5 minutes

Ingredient List:

- 2 cups ricotta cheese, crumbled
- 4 slices of bread
- ½ cup flaxseeds
- 1 tsp. rosemary
- 4 Tbsp. pomace olive oil
- Salt and pepper to taste

zzzzzzzzzzzzzzzzzzzzzzzzzzzzzzzzzzzzzzzzzzzzzzz

Instructions:

1. Combine ricotta cheese, rosemary, flaxseeds, salt, and pepper in a bowl. Mix well until all the ingredients are evenly combined. Set aside.

2. Remove the edges of bread slices. Slightly dampen each slice with water and roll them into a thin sheet with a rolling pin.

3. Take a thin sheet of bread in your and put ¼ portion of prepared cheese mix in the center. Fold the sheet in half and press the edges to seal the roll.

4. Repeat the same procedure with remaining ingredients and make 4 rolls. Keep aside.

5. Heat olive oil in a non-stick pan over medium-high flame. Put prepared rolls in the pan and shallow fry until golden-brown.

6. Once ready, place the rolls on a serving platter

7. Serve hot with ketchup!

15) Milk Flaxseed Oats

Milky oats with flaxseeds, raisins, and almonds!

Yield: 2

Prep Time: 10 minutes

Total Cook Time: 15 minutes

Ingredient List:

- 1 quart milk
- 1 cup rolled oats
- 1 cup flax meal
- Handful of raisins
- Handful of almonds, roughly chopped
- ½ cup condensed milk
- 1 Tbsp. butter

Instructions:

1. Melt the butter in a deep bottom non-stick pan over medium-high heat. Put all the ingredients in the pan.

2. Cook until the oats are completely merged with milk and the whole mix turns thick, stirring occasionally.

3. Once done, pour the oats into two bowls.

4. Serve hot!

16) Mustard Tuna Sandwich

Flax meal bread packed with tuna, mustard, and chili mayo!

Yield: 2

Prep Time: 10 minutes

Total Cook Time: 0 minutes

Ingredient List:

- 1, 5-oz. can of flaked tuna in olive oil, oil drained
- Mustard sauce
- Chili Mayonnaise
- 1 small onion, thinly sliced
- 1 small avocado, thinly sliced
- 4 slices of flax meal bread

zzzzzzzzzzzzzzzzzzzzzzzzzzzzzzzzzzzzzzzzzzzzzzzzzzz

Instructions:

1. Place a slice of bread on the chopping board. Spread 1 Tbsp. of mustard on it.

2. Then add onion slices, avocado slices, and tuna flakes. Set aside.

3. Spread 1 Tbsp. of chili mayo on another and place it over the layer of tuna flakes on chopping board.

4. Repeat the same procedure and make another sandwich.

5. Serve!

17) Flaxseed Coconut Cereal

Rice bran in coconut milk and condensed milk with shredded coconut!

Yield: 2

Prep Time: 10 minutes

Total Cook Time: 5 minutes

Ingredient List:

- 1 cup flax meal
- 3 cup coconut milk
- ½ cup shredded coconut
- 4 cups rice bran
- ½ cup condensed milk

Instructions:

1. Put all the ingredients in a deep bottom pan and mix well. Place it over medium-high heat and bring to boil. Set aside.

2. Put 2 cups of rice bran in 2 bowls. Pour over prepared mix.

3. Serve hot!

18) Ham Quiche

Chopped ham and egg whites baked together with cheddar cheese!

Yield: 2

Prep Time: 10 minutes

Total Cook Time: 20 minutes

Ingredient List:

- ½ pound ham, finely chopped
- 4 cups egg white
- 2 spring onions, finely chopped
- 1 cup flax meal
- 2 tsp. dried basil
- 1 cup cheddar cheese
- Olive oil spray for greasing
- Salt and pepper to taste

zzzzzzzzzzzzzzzzzzzzzzzzzzzzzzzzzzzzzzzzzzzzzzzzz

Instructions:

1. Preheat the oven 350 ºF.

2. Lightly grease a baking dish with olive oil spray.

3. Combine all the ingredients in a large bowl. Mix well until everything is uniformly combined.

4. Now, pour the prepared mix in a baking dish.

5. Bake for 15-20 minutes or until eggs are cooked through and a skewer inserted in the center comes out clean.

6. Once done, remove the baking dish from oven to cool down a bit.

7. Serve hot!

19) Chicken Egg Toasts

Chicken and eggs baked over bread slices with parmesan cheese!

Yield: 2

Prep Time: 15 minutes

Total Cook Time: 10 minutes

Ingredient List:

- 1 roasted chicken breast, shredded
- 1 cup parmesan cheese
- 6 slices of flax meal bread
- 3 whole organic eggs
- ½ tsp. paprika
- Olive oil spray
- Salt to taste

zzzzzzzzzzzzzzzzzzzzzzzzzzzzzzzzzzzzzzzzzzzzzzzzz

Instructions:

1. Preheat the oven 350 °F.

2. Lightly grease a baking dish with olive oil spray.

3. Combine shredded chicken, parmesan cheese, eggs, paprika, and salt in a large bowl. Mix well until all the ingredients are uniformly combined. Set aside.

4. Now, place the bread slices in prepared dish in a single layer (without overlapping each other). Pour over the prepared mix.

5. Bake for 10-15 minutes or until eggs are cooked through and a toothpick inserted in the center comes out clean.

6. Once done, remove the baking dish from oven to cool down a bit.

7. Serve hot!

Chapter IV - Main Meal

zzzzzzzzzzzzzzzzzzzzzzzzzzzzzzzzzzzzzzzzzzzzzz

20) Baked Portabella Mushrooms with Veggies

Cheese stuffed portabella mushrooms baked with veggies!

Yield: 2

Prep Time: 15 minutes

Total Cook Time: 45 minutes

Ingredient List:

- 10 portabella mushrooms, stems removed
- 1 large green bell pepper, diced
- 1 large red bell pepper, diced
- 1 large yellow bell pepper, diced
- 3 cups cottage cheese crumbled
- 1 tsp. dried rosemary
- 2 cups mozzarella cheese, shredded
- Olive oil spray
- Salt and pepper to taste

zzzzzzzzzzzzzzzzzzzzzzzzzzzzzzzzzzzzzzzzzzzzzzzzz

Instructions:

1. Preheat the oven 350 °F.

2. Lightly grease a baking dish with olive oil spray.

3. Combine cottage cheese, rosemary, salt, and pepper in a bowl. Mix well and stuff portabella mushrooms with the mixture.

4. Now, put the stuffed mushrooms and bell pepper on the prepared baking dish. Add salt and pepper Top with shredded mozzarella cheese.

5. Bake for 15-20 minutes or until the veggies are cooked through.

6. Once done, remove the tray from oven to cool down a bit.

7. Serve hot!

21) Lettuce Rolls

Battered lettuce leaves stuffed with chicken and Cajun spice!

Yield: 2

Prep Time: 30 minutes

Total Cook Time: 40 minutes

Ingredient List:

For battered lettuce

- 6 lettuce leaves
- 3 whole organic eggs
- ½ cup flax meal
- Pomace olive oil for deep frying
- Salt and pepper to taste

For filling

- ½ pound boiled and shredded chicken
- ½ cup flaxseeds
- 1 medium onion, finely chopped
- 1 tsp. Cajun spice
- 2 Tbsp. pomace olive oil
- Salt to taste

zzzzzzzzzzzzzzzzzzzzzzzzzzzzzzzzzzzzzzzzzzzzzzzzz

Instructions:

1. For battered lettuce, whisk eggs in a large bowl until frothy. Add in the flax meal, salt, and pepper. Mix well and keep aside.

2. Heat olive oil in a deep bottom pan over medium-high heat. Evenly coat each lettuce leaf with prepared egg mix and put them into the pan with hot oil (one at a time). Fry until golden but soft.

3. Once done, remove the leaves from pan with the help of a strainer. Place them on a paper towel so that it can absorb the extra oil. Keep aside.

4. For filling, heat olive oil in a non-stick pan over medium-high heat. Add all the ingredients to the pan and cook for few minutes.

5. Once done, remove the pan from heat and set aside.

6. Now, place a battered lettuce on a chopping board. Put 1/6 part of the prepared chicken mix at one of the edge and roll that edge towards the opposite edge. Seal the roll with a toothpick.

7. Repeat the same method and make 6 rolls,

8. Once ready, place the rolls on a serving platter.

9. Serve hot with mayo!

22) Pinto Bean Toasts

Baked bread with Mexican pinto beans and mozzarella cheese!

Yield: 6

Prep Time: 15 minutes

Total Cook Time: 10 minutes

Ingredient List:

- 3 cups canned Mexican pinto beans
- 3 cups mozzarella cheese, shredded
- 6 slices of flax meal bread
- 6 tsp. butter
- Salt and pepper to taste

zzzzzzzzzzzzzzzzzzzzzzzzzzzzzzzzzzzzzzzzzzzzzzzzzzz

Instructions:

1. Preheat the oven 350 °F.

2. Lightly grease a baking tray with olive oil spray.

3. Combine mozzarella cheese, salt, and pepper in a bowl. Mix well and keep aside.

4. Spread a tsp. of butter on a bread slice. Then, add a layer of pinto beans and sprinkle mozzarella cheese on the top. Repeat the same method and make 6 pieces of toast.

5. Then, place them on the prepared baking tray.

6. Bake for 5-10 minutes or until cheese melts completely.

7. Once done, remove the tray from oven to cool down a bit.

8. Serve hot!

23) Avocado Burger

Stir fried beef and veggies between avocado slices!

Yield: 2

Prep Time: 15 minutes

Total Cook Time: 10 minutes

Ingredient List:

- 2 large avocados, peeled and halved (lengthways)
- ½ pound ground beef
- ½ cup flax meal
- 1 tsp. garlic paste
- 1 tsp. soy sauce
- 2 leaves of lettuce
- 4 thin slices of tomato
- 2 thin slices of onion
- 2 Tbsp. mayonnaises
- 2 Tbsp. pomace olive oil
- Salt and pepper to taste

zzzzzzzzzzzzzzzzzzzzzzzzzzzzzzzzzzzzzzzzzzzzzzzzzz

Instructions:

1. Combine beef, flax meal, garlic paste, soy sauce, salt, and pepper in a large bowl. Mix well until evenly combined. Divide the mix into two equal portions and make 2 oval shaped patties. Set aside.

2. Heat the oil in a non-stick pan over medium-high flame. Put the prepared patties into the pan with hot oil and fry both sides until golden-brown and done.

3. Once done, remove the patties from pan and set aside.

4. Now, place a half slice of avocado on a chopping board and put the fried patty on it. Add a lettuce leaf, some tomato slices, some onion slices, and a little mayo. Top it with the other half of the avocado.

5. Repeat the same method and assemble another avocado burger.

6. Serve!

24) Potato Pork Scramble

A delicious scramble of minced pork, potatoes, and eggs!

Yield: 2

Prep Time: 15 minutes

Total Cook Time: 30 minutes

Ingredient List:

- 1 pound minced pork
- 2 medium boiled potatoes, diced
- 1 large onion, finely chopped
- ½ cup flax seeds
- 1 tsp. freshly grated ginger
- 2 tsp. freshly grated garlic
- 1 tsp. fresh chives, finely chopped
- 4 whole organic eggs
- 2 Tbsp. pomace olive oil
- Salt and pepper to taste

zzzzzzzzzzzzzzzzzzzzzzzzzzzzzzzzzzzzzzzzzzzzzzz

Instructions:

1. Heat olive oil in a deep bottom pan over medium-high heat. Stir in chopped onion and sauté until golden-brown. Add grated ginger and garlic to the pan. Cook for few minutes while stirring occasionally.

2. Whisk eggs in a large bowl until frothy and set aside.

3. Now, add minced pork, potatoes, flaxseeds, chives, pepper, and salt to the pan. Cook until pork is cooked through and turns golden brown.

4. Then, add the whisked eggs to the pan and cook until eggs are done.

5. Once ready, transfer the scramble to a serving bowl.

6. Serve hot with bread and steamed veggies.

25) Stir Fried Teriyaki Salmon with Toasted Flaxseeds

Salmon and white button mushrooms in sweet teriyaki sauce. Topped with toasted flaxseeds and spring onion!

Yield: 2

Prep Time: 20 minutes

Total Cook Time: 30 minutes

Ingredient List:

- 1 pound salmon, diced
- 2 cups white button mushrooms, chopped
- 1 large onion, diced
- 1 tsp. garlic powder
- 1 tsp. dried sage
- ½ cup flaxseeds
- Stem of 1 spring onion, finely chopped (for garnishing)
- 1 Tbsp. teriyaki sauce
- 2 Tbsp. pomace olive oil

zzzzzzzzzzzzzzzzzzzzzzzzzzzzzzzzzzzzzzzzzzzzzzzzzz

Instructions:

1. Heat oil in a non-stick pan over medium-high heat. Stir in the onion and mushrooms. Cook them a few seconds.

2. Then add in garlic powder, dried sage, pepper and salt. Mix well and then cook for a minute. Add in the diced salmon and 2 cups of water and cover the pan with a lid and let it simmer over low heat until the fish is done.

3. Once done, remove the pan from heat and add teriyaki sauce to the pan. Mix well and transfer the fish to a serving platter. Set aside.

4. Heat a pan over medium-high heat. Add in flaxseeds and roast until crisp. Put toasted flaxseeds over the prepared fish.

5. Garnish with chopped spring onion.

6. Serve hot with garlic bread!

26) Chorizo Flaxseed Curry

Chorizo in onion and tomato curry with curry masala!

Yield: 2

Prep Time: 20 minutes

Total Cook Time: 30 minutes

Ingredient List:

- ½ pound chorizo
- 1 large onion, finely chopped
- 2 cups tomato puree
- 2 tsp. freshly grated ginger
- 4 Tbsp. flaxseeds
- 1 tsp. curry masala
- Handful of fresh coriander leaves
- 2 Tbsp. mustard oil
- Salt to taste

zzzzzzzzzzzzzzzzzzzzzzzzzzzzzzzzzzzzzzzzzzzzzzzzz

Instructions:

1. Heat olive oil in a deep bottom pan over medium-high heat. Stir in chopped onion and sauté until golden-brown. Add grated ginger to the pan. Cook for few minutes while stirring occasionally.

2. Now, add tomato puree, curry masala, and salt to the pan. Cook until the whole mixt turns into thick gravy.

3. Add in chorizo, flax seeds, and one pint of water. Stir and cover the pan with its lid. Let it simmer over low heat until the water reduces to half.

4. Once done, remove the pan from heat and transfer the curry to a serving bowl.

5. Garnish with fresh coriander leaves.

6. Serve hot with boiled rice or naan bread.

27) Baked Aubergine

Soft and mushy aubergine stuffed with three cheese!

Yield: 2

Prep Time: 15 minutes

Total Cook Time: 15 minutes

Ingredient List:

- 1 large aubergine, head removed and halved (lengthways)
- 1 cup mozzarella cheese
- 1 cup cheddar cheese
- 1 cup parmesan cheese
- ½ cup flaxseeds
- 1 cup canned jalapeno slices
- Olive oil spray
- Salt and pepper to taste

zzzzzzzzzzzzzzzzzzzzzzzzzzzzzzzzzzzzzzzzzzzzzzzzz

Instructions:

1. Preheat the oven 350 ºF.

2. Lightly grease a baking tray with olive oil spray.

3. Combine mozzarella cheese, cheddar cheese, parmesan cheese, flaxseeds, jalapeno slices, salt, and pepper in a large bowl. Mix well and set aside.

4. Scoop out the pulp from each half of the aubergine. Stuff the aubergine shells with prepared cheese mix.

5. Place them on the prepared baking tray and spray some olive oil over them.

6. Bake for 10-15 minutes or until cheese melts down completely.

7. Once done, remove the tray from oven to cool down a bit.

8. Serve hot!

28) Fried Chicken Fillet

Chicken breast battered with eggs and flax meal!

Yield: 1

Prep Time: 10 minutes

Total Cook Time: 10 minutes

Ingredient List:

- ½ pound chicken breast, boneless and skinless
- ½ cup flax meal
- 2 whole organic eggs
- ½ tsp. paprika
- 1 tsp. garlic paste
- 1 tsp. dried oregano
- Pomace olive oil
- Salt to taste

zzzzzzzzzzzzzzzzzzzzzzzzzzzzzzzzzzzzzzzzzzzzzzz

Instructions:

1. Combine flax meal, eggs, paprika, garlic paste, oregano, and salt in a large bowl. Mix well until all the ingredients are uniformly combined. Keep aside.

2. Heat olive oil in a deep bottom pan over medium-high heat. Evenly coat the chicken breast with prepared egg mix and put it into the pan. Fry until golden-brown and crisp.

3. Once done, remove the chicken fillet from pan with the help of a strainer and place it on a paper towel so that it can absorb the extra oil. Keep aside.

4. Serve hot with fried rice or bread.

29) Beef Taco

Flax meal taco filled with stir fried minced beef and veggies!

Yield: 2

Prep Time: 15 minutes

Total Cook Time: 30 minutes

Ingredient List:

- 4 flax meal tortillas
- 1 pound minced beef
- ½ cup flax meal
- 2 tsp. freshly grated garlic
- 2 tsp. soy sauce
- 1 cup lettuce, chopped
- 1 medium tomato, chopped
- 1 medium onion, chopped
- 2 Tbsp. mayonnaises
- 2 Tbsp. pomace olive oil
- Salt and pepper to taste

zzzzzzzzzzzzzzzzzzzzzzzzzzzzzzzzzzzzzzzzzzzzzzzzzz

Instructions:

1. Heat oil in a non-stick pan over medium-high flame. Put beef, garlic, soy sauce, salt, and pepper in the pan. Cook until golden-brown and done.

2. Once done, remove the pan from heat and set aside.

3. Now, heat the flax meal tortilla in a pan over medium-high heat.

4. Then, place a tortilla on a chopping board. Put a ¼ portion of the prepared mix in the center. Add some lettuce, tomatoes, and onion. Top with mayo and fold the taco into half.

5. Repeat the same method and assemble 4 tacos.

6. Serve!

Chapter V – Soups

zzzzzzzzzzzzzzzzzzzzzzzzzzzzzzzzzzzzzzzzzzzzzzzzz

30) Chicken Cream Soup

Shredded roasted chicken breast in sour cream soup!

Yield: 2

Prep Time: 10 minutes

Total Cook Time: 30 minutes

Ingredient List:

- ½ pound roasted chicken breast, shredded
- 1 cup flax meal
- 1 quart chicken stock
- 1 cup sour cream
- Salt and pepper to taste

zzzzzzzzzzzzzzzzzzzzzzzzzzzzzzzzzzzzzzzzzzzzzzzz

Instructions:

1. Put all the ingredients in a deep bottom pan and add in a quart of water. Cover the pan with a lid.

2. Let it simmer over low heat until the liquid reduces by half.

3. Once ready, remove the pan from heat and pour the soup into two bowls.

4. Serve hot with soup sticks.

31) Beef Rice Soup

Minced beef and rice cooked with vegetable stock!

Yield: 2

Prep Time: 10 minutes

Total Cook Time: 30 minutes

Ingredient List:

- ½ pound minced beef
- 1 cup rice, rinsed
- 1 cup flax meal
- 1 ½ quart vegetable stock
- Salt and pepper to taste

zzzzzzzzzzzzzzzzzzzzzzzzzzzzzzzzzzzzzzzzzzzzzzzzzzz

Instructions:

1. Put all the ingredients in a deep bottom pan and add in a quart of water. Cover the pan with a lid.

2. Let it simmer over low heat until the beef and rice done.

3. Once ready, remove the pan from heat and pour the soup into two bowls.

4. Serve hot with soup sticks.

32) Flaxseed Tomato Soup

Thick tomato soup with ginger and dried basil!

Yield: 3

Prep Time: 5 minutes

Total Cook Time: 30 minutes

Ingredient List:

- ½ quart tomato puree
- 1 cup flax seeds
- 1 tsp. freshly grated ginger
- 2 tsp. dried basil
- 2 Tbsp. butter
- Salt and pepper to taste

zzzzzzzzzzzzzzzzzzzzzzzzzzzzzzzzzzzzzzzzzzzzzzz

Instructions:

1. Put all the ingredients in a deep bottom pan and add in a quart of water. Cover the pan with a lid.

2. Let it simmer over low heat until the liquid reduces by half.

3. Once ready, remove the pan from heat and pour the soup into three bowls.

4. Serve hot with soup sticks.

33) Pork Mushroom Soup

Diced pork and white button mushrooms cooked in vegetable stock!

Yield: 2

Prep Time: 10 minutes

Total Cook Time: 45 minutes

Ingredient List:

- ½ pound pork, diced into bite size pieces
- 2 cups white button mushrooms, chopped
- 1 cup flax meal
- 2 quarts vegetable stock
- Salt and pepper to taste

Instructions:

1. Put all the ingredients in a deep bottom pan and add in a quart of water. Cover the pan with a lid.

2. Let it simmer over low heat until pork is cooked through and the liquid reduces by half.

3. Once ready, remove the pan from heat and pour the soup into two bowls.

4. Serve hot with soup sticks.

34) Thai Tofu Bell Pepper Soup

Tofu and bell peppers in Thai curry paste soup!

Yield: 2

Prep Time: 15 minutes

Total Cook Time: 30 minutes

Ingredient List:

- 1 large red bell pepper, diced
- 1 large yellow bell pepper, diced
- ½ pound tofu, diced
- 2 spring onions, finely chopped
- 3 Tbsp. Thai curry paste
- 1 cup flax meal
- 2 Tbsp. butter
- Salt and pepper to taste

zzzzzzzzzzzzzzzzzzzzzzzzzzzzzzzzzzzzzzzzzzzzzzzzzz

Instructions:

1. Put all the ingredients in a deep bottom pan and add in a quart of water. Cover the pan with a lid.

2. Let it simmer over low heat until bell peppers are done and the liquid reduces by half.

3. Once ready, remove the pan from heat and pour the soup into two bowls.

4. Serve hot with soup sticks.

Chapter VI – Desserts

zzzzzzzzzzzzzzzzzzzzzzzzzzzzzzzzzzzzzzzzzzzzzzzzz

35) Coffee Flaxseed Pie

Cream cheese coffee flavored pie with flaxseeds and butter base!

Yield: 6

Prep Time: 10 minutes

Total Cook Time: 5 minutes

Ingredient List:

- 3 cups cream
- Gelatin
- 1 cup brown sugar
- 1 Tbsp. coffee
- 2 cups flax meal
- ½ cup butter

zzzzzzzzzzzzzzzzzzzzzzzzzzzzzzzzzzzzzzzzzzzzzzzz

Instructions:

1. Combine the butter and flax meal in a bowl. Transfer the mix to a baking dish and pat down the mixture with a spoon in an even layer.

2. Now, refrigerate the mix for an hour.

3. In the meantime, combine water and gelatin in a sauce pan. Once thick, place the sauce pan over low heat until gelatine dissolves completely. Let it cool down a bit (do not let it set).

4. No, blend cream and brown sugar with a hand blender until thick. Add in gelatine and coffee. Again, blend until uniformly combined.

5. Take out flax meal and butter mix from the refrigerator and pour the prepared mix over it. Refrigerate until set.

6. Once set, take out the tray from refrigerator and cut it slices with a knife.

7. Serve!

36) Fruit Cream

Assorted fruits in whipped cream and condensed milk mix!

Yield: 6

Prep Time: 15 minutes

Total Cook Time: 0 minutes

Ingredient List:

- 2 cups whipped cream
- 1 cup flax meal
- 1 cup grapes
- 1 cup strawberries, chopped
- 1 cup pineapple, chopped
- 1 cup apple, chopped
- 1 cup cherries, deseeded
- 1 cup almonds, roughly chopped
- 2 tsp. vanilla essence
- 2 cups condensed milk

zzzzzzzzzzzzzzzzzzzzzzzzzzzzzzzzzzzzzzzzzzzzzzzzzz

Instructions:

1. Combine, all the ingredients in a large bowl. Mix well and refrigerate for an hour.

2. Serve!

37) Fruit Cupcakes

Cupcakes filled with assorted and almonds!

Yield: 6

Prep Time: 30 minutes

Total Cook Time: 15 minutes

Ingredient List:

- 2 whole organic eggs
- 3 cups flax meal
- 1 cup pineapple, chopped
- 1 cup apple, chopped
- 1 cup cherries, deseeded
- 1 cup almonds, roughly chopped
- 2 tsp. pineapple essence
- 1 cup milk
- 2 tsp. baking powder
- 2 cups condensed milk
- ½ cup butter
- Butter for greasing

zzzzzzzzzzzzzzzzzzzzzzzzzzzzzzzzzzzzzzzzzzzzzzzz

Instructions:

1. Preheat the oven 350 °F.

2. Lightly grease 6 muffin molds with butter.

3. Combine all the ingredients in a large bowl. Mix well until all the ingredients are uniformly combined.

4. Then, pour prepared mix into the molds and place them on a baking tray.

5. Bake for 10-15 minutes or until a skewer inserted in the center comes out clean.

6. Once done, remove the baking tray from oven allow it to cool down a bit.

7. Serve warm!

38) Banana Pecan Ice-cream

Banana, pecan, and whipped cream ice-cream with flaxseeds!

Yield: 4

Prep Time: 10 minutes

Total Cook Time: 0 minutes

Ingredient List:

- 4 large bananas, diced
- ½ cup brown sugar
- 1 cup flaxseeds
- 1 whipped cream
- 1 tsp. vanilla essence
- 1 cup pecans, roughly chopped

zzzzzzzzzzzzzzzzzzzzzzzzzzzzzzzzzzzzzzzzzzzzzzzzzz

Instructions:

1. Blend all the ingredients in a blender until smooth.

2. Pour the mixture in a box and cover it with a lid.

3. Freeze for 4-5 hours.

4. Serve!

39) Flaxseed Caramel Toffee

Flaxseeds and caramel toffee with peanuts!

Yield: 6

Prep Time: 10 minutes

Total Cook Time: 5 minutes

Ingredient List:

- 2 cups brown sugar
- 2 cup flax meal
- 1 cup butter
- 1 cup peanuts, roughly chopped
- ½ tsp. salt

zzzzzzzzzzzzzzzzzzzzzzzzzzzzzzzzzzzzzzzzzzzzzzzzz

Instructions:

1. Combine half cup butter and flax meal in a bowl. Transfer the mix to a baking dish and pat down the mixture with a spoon in an even layer.

2. Now, refrigerate the mix for an hour.

3. In the meantime, melt the remaining butter in a sauce pan. Add in the sugar and salt. Cook until sugar melts down completely and the whole mixture turns thick.

4. Take out flax meal and butter mix from the refrigerator and pour the prepared caramel over it. Then, sprinkle peanuts over it and refrigerate for another hour.

5. Once set, take out the tray from refrigerator and cut it into pieces with a knife.

6. Serve!

Chapter VII - Shakes

zzzzzzzzzzzzzzzzzzzzzzzzzzzzzzzzzzzzzzzzzzzzzzzzzzzz

40) Pineapple Shake

Pineapple pieces blended with milk and flaxseeds!

Yield: 2

Prep Time: 5 minutes

Total Cook Time: 0 minutes

Ingredient List:

- 3 cups milk
- 3 cups pineapple, chopped
- 2 Tbsp. flaxseeds
- 1 cup condensed milk

zzzzzzzzzzzzzzzzzzzzzzzzzzzzzzzzzzzzzzzzzzzzzzzzzz

Instructions:

1. Blend all the ingredients in a food processor until smooth.
2. Serve!

41) Cherry Shake

Cherries and milk blended together with flaxseeds!

Yield: 2

Prep Time: 5 minutes

Total Cook Time: 0 minutes

Ingredient List:

- 3 cups milk
- 3 cups cherries, deseeded
- 2 Tbsp. flaxseeds
- 1 cup condensed milk

zzzzzzzzzzzzzzzzzzzzzzzzzzzzzzzzzzzzzzzzzzzzzzzzzz

Instructions:

1. Blend all the ingredients in a food processor until smooth.
2. Serve!

42) Mango Shake

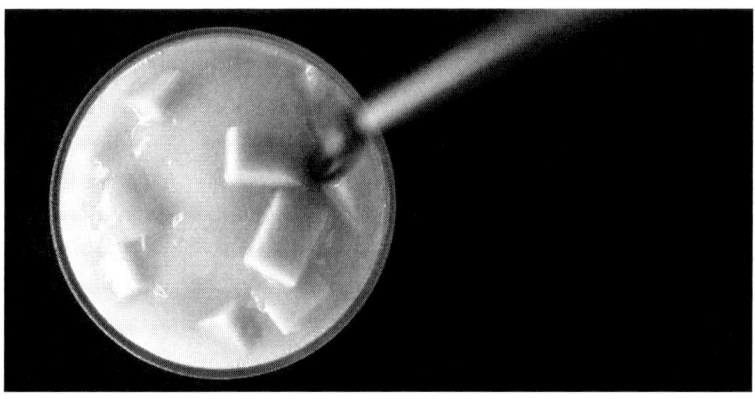

Mango and milk blended together with condensed milk!

Yield: 2

Prep Time: 5 minutes

Total Cook Time: 0 minutes

Ingredient List:

- 3 cups milk
- 3 cups mango, chopped
- 2 Tbsp. flaxseeds
- 1 cup condensed milk

zzzzzzzzzzzzzzzzzzzzzzzzzzzzzzzzzzzzzzzzzzzzzzzzzz

Instructions:

1. Blend all the ingredients in a food processor until smooth.

2. Serve!

43) Butterscotch Shake

Butterscotch ice cream and milk blended together!

Yield: 2

Prep Time: 5 minutes

Total Cook Time: 0 minutes

Ingredient List:

- ½ quart milk
- 2 scoops of butter scotch ice-cream
- 2 Tbsp. flaxseeds
- 1 cup condensed milk

zzzzzzzzzzzzzzzzzzzzzzzzzzzzzzzzzzzzzzzzzzzzzzzzzz

Instructions:

1. Blend all the ingredients a food processor until smooth.
2. Serve!

44) Banana Shake

Bananas blended with milk and flaxseeds!

Yield: 2

Prep Time: 5 minutes

Total Cook Time: 0 minutes

Ingredient List:

- 3 cups milk
- 2 large bananas, chopped
- 2 Tbsp. flaxseeds
- 1 cup condensed milk

ZZZZZZZZZZZZZZZZZZZZZZZZZZZZZZZZZZZZZZZZZZZZZZZZZZZZ

Instructions:

1. Blend all the ingredients in a food processor until smooth.
2. Serve!

Chapter VIII - Smoothies

zzzzzzzzzzzzzzzzzzzzzzzzzzzzzzzzzzzzzzzzzzzzzzzzzzz

45) Pineapple Kiwi Smoothie

Pineapple, kiwi, and banana blended together with flaxseeds!

Yield: 2

Prep Time: 5 minutes

Total Cook Time: 0 minutes

Ingredient List:

- 2 cups pineapple, chopped
- 2 cups kiwi fruit, chopped
- 1 large banana, chopped
- 2 Tbsp. flaxseeds

zzzzzzzzzzzzzzzzzzzzzzzzzzzzzzzzzzzzzzzzzzzzzzzzzzz

Instructions:

1. Blend all the ingredients in a food processor until smooth.

2. Serve!

46) Plum Mango Smoothie

Plums, mango, and banana blended with flaxseeds!

Yield: 2

Prep Time: 5 minutes

Total Cook Time: 0 minutes

Ingredient List:

- 2 cups plum, chopped
- 2 cups mango, chopped
- 1 large banana, chopped
- 2 Tbsp. flaxseeds

zzzzzzzzzzzzzzzzzzzzzzzzzzzzzzzzzzzzzzzzzzzzzzzzzz

Instructions:

1. Blend all the ingredients in a food processor until smooth.

2. Serve!

47) Banana Apple Smoothie

Banana and apples blended together with flaxseeds!

Yield: 2

Prep Time: 5 minutes

Total Cook Time: 0 minutes

Ingredient List:

- 3 large bananas, chopped
- 2 medium apples, chopped
- 2 Tbsp. flaxseeds

zzzzzzzzzzzzzzzzzzzzzzzzzzzzzzzzzzzzzzzzzzzzzzzzzz

Instructions:

1. Blend all the ingredients in a food processor until smooth.

2. Serve!

48) Passion Fruit Grape Smoothie

Passion fruit and grapes blended with banana!

Yield: 2

Prep Time: 5 minutes

Total Cook Time: 0 minutes

Ingredient List:

- 2 cups passion fruit, chopped
- 2 cups black grapes
- 1 large banana, chopped
- 2 Tbsp. flaxseeds

zzzzzzzzzzzzzzzzzzzzzzzzzzzzzzzzzzzzzzzzzzzzzzzzzz

Instructions:

1. Blend all the ingredients in a food processor until smooth.

2. Serve!

49) Very Berry Smoothie

Strawberries, blueberries, blackberries, raspberries blended with banana!

Yield: 2

Prep Time: 5 minutes

Total Cook Time: 0 minutes

Ingredient List:

- 1 cup blueberries, chopped
- 1 cup strawberries, chopped1 cup raspberries
- 1 cup blackberries
- 1 large banana, chopped
- 2 Tbsp. flaxseeds

zzzzzzzzzzzzzzzzzzzzzzzzzzzzzzzzzzzzzzzzzzzzzz

Instructions:

1. Blend all the ingredients in a food processor until smooth.

2. Serve!

About the Author

A native of Albuquerque, New Mexico, Sophia Freeman found her calling in the culinary arts when she enrolled at the Sante Fe School of Cooking. Freeman decided to take a year after graduation and travel around Europe, sampling the cuisine from small bistros and family owned restaurants from Italy to Portugal. Her bubbly personality and inquisitive nature made her popular with the locals in the villages and when she finished her trip and came home, she had made friends for life in the places she had visited. She also came home with a deeper understanding of European cuisine.

Freeman went to work at one of Albuquerque's 5-star restaurants as a sous-chef and soon worked her way up to head chef. The restaurant began to feature Freeman's original dishes as specials on the menu and soon after, she began to write e-books with her recipes. Sophia's dishes mix local flavours with European inspiration making them irresistible to the diners in her restaurant and the online community.

Freeman's experience in Europe didn't just teach her new ways of cooking, but also unique methods of presentation. Using rich sauces, crisp vegetables and meat cooked to perfection, she creates a stunning display as well as a delectable dish. She has won many local awards for her cuisine and she continues to delight her diners with her culinary masterpieces.

Author's Afterthoughts

I want to convey my big thanks to all of my readers who have taken the time to read my book. Readers like you make my work so rewarding and I cherish each and every one of you.

Grateful cannot describe how I feel when I know that someone has chosen my work over all of the choices available online. I hope you enjoyed the book as much as I enjoyed writing it.

Feedback from my readers is how I grow and learn as a chef and an author. Please take the time to let me know your thoughts by leaving a review on Amazon so I and your fellow readers can learn from your experience.

My deepest thanks,

Sophia Freeman

https://sophia.subscribemenow.com/

Manufactured by Amazon.ca
Acheson, AB